the myth of your misfit

making meaning

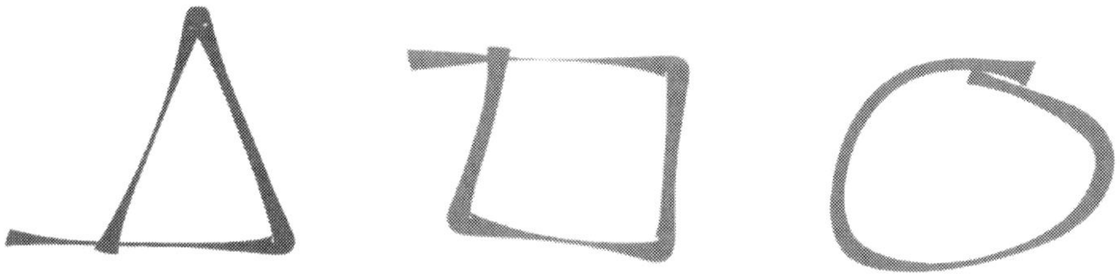

the myth
of your misfit

making meaning

barbara allyn

Editing by Michael Christopher Duguay

Tribal Theory Arts + Sciences
www.tribaltheory.org

ISBN: 978-0-9952514-0-3
ISBN-13: 978-0-9952514-0-3

TO KAY, MAY, DAISY, MAISIE, BILL, GUY AND REG
MY ELDERS WHO LOVED, ENCOURAGED AND GUIDED ME TO
CREATE MY OWN PATH.

TO MADISON, JOSHUA
AND
FRANK
WHO LOVINGLY ACCEPT AND CARE FOR ME
EVERY DAY
IN EVERY WAY.

TO MY CRISIS COMPANIONS, WHOM I HOLD IN THE HIGHEST
REGARD.

YOU HAVE ALL GIVEN ME A SAFE PLACE TO BELONG, AND I AM
FOREVER GRATEFUL.

CONTENTS

Acknowledgements
Introduction
About This Book

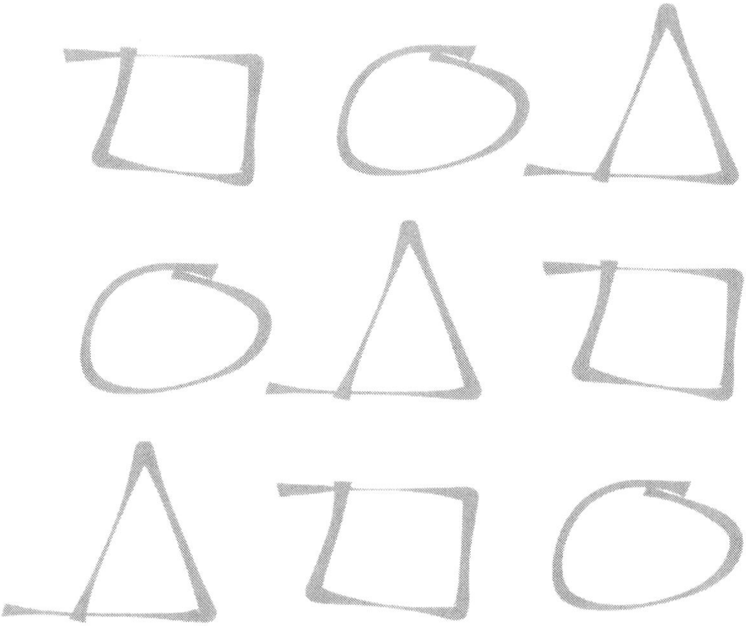

ACKNOWLEDGMENTS

I am grateful to everyone I have ever met in my life. Like the music that lies between the notes, you are the space between the words and lines in this book. You are my Tribe.

To my big sister Susan Hutchinson, who helped me shape an amorphous clump of ideas into this book and believed in me with all her heart.

To my gifted editor, Michael Christopher Duguay for his wise council.

With gratitude and love to my dear friends who have always stood beside me and encouraged me to keep moving forward:

Deanne Sweeney, Cameron MacKay, Jen Williams,
Allyson Ryder, Susanne & Jessica Külmorgen-Hille,
Christie Christie, Sara Pedersen, Valerie Henrich, Beth Denning,
Rhonda Lee McIsaac, Sue Simpson, Rinat De Picciotto,
Richard Kramer, Saxony Brown, Amy Byrne, Nic Mitch,
Michael Canning, Sylvie Morgan, Katie, Patricia & Aaron Fenton,
Kevin Daum, Jeremy Edward Brink, Al Wylie & Kim Gibson,
May Shihadeh, Evelyn Larsen, Nicole Miller, Rae Zikloi,
Jordan Malm, Gordon Langill, Anne Pick & Bill Spahic,
Jean Ellis, Sandra VanderHaven Boulianne.

To Nick Trusolino for your inspiration and support.

To my fellow Hunter and amazing Tribal Theory partner Melissa van der Maden, for taking a leap of faith.

To Erica Siddall, the Homebody, for her enthusiasm and contributions.

To Johnny and Sally Flowers, for your spirit and wisdom.

To my brother, Bill (Dubber) Hutchinson who, throughout some of my toughest times, has always been there. Truly the best loving big brother a sister could ask for.

To Lesley Brown and her family who continually open their door to welcome me, with offerings of amazing food, caring company, and a lovely feeling of home.

To Sandra Bloom, whose work, The Sanctuary Model, changed the way I move in the world,

To Patsy De Courcy Ireland, who from the moment I walked into her class on crisis and trauma, blessed my life, by being my mentor and friend.

With deep appreciation to my husband, Frank, the most truly accepting and loving person I know, for morning coffees and insightful discussion, making me laugh and having faith in us.

To my children, I love you to the MOON and back again.

"If you weren't you, then we'd all be a bit less, um …
we"

A.A. Milne

INTRODUCTION

I stood at the door of my office and looked down the hall to the waiting room. Another hour was coming to an end, and the doors of several other offices opened as our adolescent clients completed their counselling sessions.

I often experienced sadness at this hourly ritual. The body language and facial expressions of our young clients often left me with the impression that they felt as though they were misfits.

This day, however, as my next young client walked toward me, adorned in tattoos, ears and nose pierced, the scars of self-harm marking her collar bones, I observed something different. What I saw was a 'tribal' person. Her body told a different/new story. It elucidated who she now had become; a proclamation of her right to exist, marking her place in her Tribe.

In that flash of recognition, it became clear to me that those behaviours and symptoms which my colleagues and I routinely interpreted and treated as disorders, dysfunctions, and diseases were, in fact, natural and often creative expressions of a deeper and more fundamental need which was not being met; the need to understand, and subsequently live, from our authentic place in our Tribe.

My 'tribal' youth entered my office. I shut the door, took a marker to my whiteboard, and drew three circles within one another. In the outer circle I wrote 'Hunter', in the middle circle 'Guard', and in the inner circle, 'Homebody'. At the top of the board I wrote (and underlined) 'Your Tribe'.

In the session that unfolded, this simple drawing of three circles came alive with meaning for both of us. Together, my young client and I explored where she felt she would belong if she were to belong to a Tribe. Our discoveries that session would prove to be transformative.

For the subsequent decade, I have employed these three circles and the tribal approach, which I have named Tribal Theory, working in crisis response, trauma, as well as clinical and family work. It has proven indispensable in frontline crisis work, mediation, workshops, training and counselling; to social workers, first responders, medical and military workers, parents, teachers, and families, and in innumerable coffee shop chats with all who have shown interest.

What has emerged has been an almost universally accepted framework which has allowed a better understanding of ourselves and others. By 're-visioning' our place in our tribe through the lens of Tribal Theory, our relationships and stories of ourselves and others in community life are renewed and revitalized. It provides a broader and deeper explanation of how our responses to trauma have affected us personally and globally.

I, as well as others, have experienced the beginning of spiritual, psychological, and even physical healing within moments of being introduced to this theory. Tribal Theory can initiate a rapid but enduring shift in how people see themselves and others; A shift away from blame and shame towards an understanding and appreciation of the value of one another. We accept our place in the Tribe and begin to value our unique being.

Tribal Theory is not about 'being disordered', but looking at the source of the pain - which is 'being displaced'. When displaced, we present ourselves with maladaptive behaviours and dysfunctions both in mind and in body. Behaviours are clues. What we commonly called disorders are, more accurately, symptoms of a larger problem: displacement. To understand each personal story of displacement is to find a map toward personal healing.

When one discovers the myth of one's misfit, a distinct compulsion to express one's natural gifts creatively and make meaning of one's life story naturally follows. It is the genesis of a new meaning that is the key to healing, resilience, and post-traumatic growth.

THE MYTH OF YOUR MISFIT

ABOUT THIS BOOK

You are part of your Tribe. Your story plays an important role in understanding Tribal Theory. This book is designed to be interactive so that you can reflect and consider while you read. In the writing of this book, I have tried to communicate the concepts of Tribal Theory in the same everyday language and structure from which it evolved.

The Myth of Your Misfit is a place for you to discover, and even play with the story of who you are. There are blank journal pages throughout this book for your own notes, ideas, and thoughts, and even the personal stories of others that may inspire you in re-telling your own.

You are encouraged to bring all of you to the table while you interact with this book and learn about Tribal Theory. Explore your authentic role in your Tribe, and re-construct your story in order to celebrate who you are. Learn about how others in the Tribe respond, and use this new awareness as a guide to help you to understand the actions taken by those around you.

There are tribal stories and case studies to help illustrate basic concepts. There are tales of applied Tribal Theory, contributed by those who have used it. The stories are real, but have been modified so as not to identify the participants.

There are also pages marked 'Walkabout'. These are the breadcrumbs of ideas that have evolved alongside Tribal Theory and that are designed to lead towards and enhance its meaning.

When people are introduced to Tribal Theory, they quickly tap into it, using intuition and strategies they have already learned in everyday life. They begin to see others with new eyes. Tribal Theory helps them to recognize that an alternative story of who they are can exist. Not the story told to them by others, (the ones who have suggested that they are not worthy, or enough, or capable), but the story of who they really are and the unique gifts that they bring to the world.

Tribal Theory helps people identify their authentic selves and their place in their social Tribe. When you discover your place, where you belong, you discover a new wisdom, freedom, and creativity.

Making meaning of your life stories puts the puzzle together. A new picture emerges and a new understanding begins. Tribal Theory is the framework but the story is written by you.

TRIBAL THEORY

TRIBAL THEORY

'Home is not where you were born, home is where your attempts to escape cease' - Naguib Mahfouz

THE TRIBE

We are all born into the Human Social Tribe.
As a Member of the Tribe, each of us is celebrated for our natural gifts and abilities and encouraged to assume the role that fits with our truest, authentic self. Although roles in the Tribe differ, each person is valued and needed. When one is able to live in and from their authentic role in the Tribe, they feel a sense of ease, order, and place.
They belong.

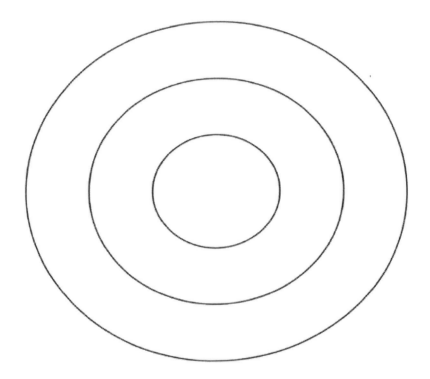

THE TRIBAL CIRCLES

The three circles represent the primal roles in a Tribe.

With each of these roles come characteristics and ways of being that contribute to the survival of the Tribe. Each of us has our primal place in the Tribe, a place where we best fit. When we are rooted in our primal place in the Tribe, we flourish.

The transformative power of Tribal Theory first reveals itself when you begin to identify your authentic role.

The two foundational roles in the Tribe are the Hunter, represented by the outer circle, and the Homebody, drawn as the inner circle. The middle circle is the Guard. The Guard is a circumstantially 'evoked' role, a part of both the Hunter and the Homebody, that is accessed or 'called into being' when a real or perceived threat from an environment occurs, and a protector is required. The Guard role will be explored in further depth later in the book.

For now, let's look at the respective roles of the Hunter and the Homebody.

HOW DO I KNOW IF I AM A HUNTER OR A HOMEBODY?

The discovery of one's authentic role can be instantaneous for some, and require more exploration for others. As you read, consider the activities you loved as a child. Perhaps you enjoyed exploring the outdoors and wildlife, making colourful crafts, riding your bike down steep hills, or making intricate indoor reading forts out of blankets.

Try to remember where you most distinctly felt that you were being you, where your sense of wonder and curiosity seemed most alive, where you felt a sense of safety and a full sense of presence.

For those who have blurred memories of childhood, this may be more of an exploration. Just see what resonates naturally.

THE AUTHENTIC HUNTER

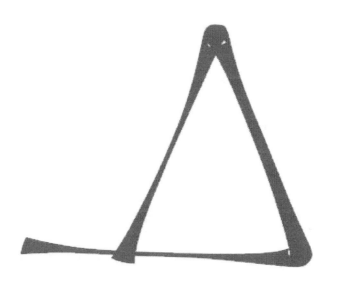

A D H D

Attention Directed in a Higher Dimension

THE AUTHENTIC HUNTER

NATURE & SPIRIT

"not all those that wander are lost"

J.R.R. Tolkien

A Hunter's Tale

I don't know why, but I couldn't stand sitting at my desk in middle school. I would rush, on the first day of school, to grab a seat by the window. In fact, I would worry for nights in anticipation of that first day, anxiously preparing how I was going to beat my classmates to a window desk. I would do practice runs from my front door to the school, timing myself, while guessing which class I would be in and how long it would take to get there. I would open my window at night and consciously try to send my feelings of being trapped in school again out the window while taking big whiffs of the fall leaves outside. That smell made me feel better. To this day, I purposely scope out places that feel open, whether it be a bus seat, restaurant table, office desk or place in a crowd and I still run a lot, in the woods by a creek.

First year university student diagnosed with ADHD

The Hunter embraces instinctive tracking, hunting, and survival skills to meet the essential nourishment of the Tribe. Naturally gifted with ADHD – Attention Directed in a Higher Dimension - a Hunter is restless, always moving, and resting only long enough to move again. Hunters are born with an innate, spiritual understanding of, and connection with, nature. Hunters respond in movement. Hunters provide the energy needed to survive. Hunters are story makers.

Most of us have experienced a person who won't sit still. The student in the classroom is a great example. One of the telling characteristics of a Hunter is that, without being able to 'move towards something' and literally use 'hunting' strategies in daily life, school, work, and play, these individuals experience a sense of being trapped. Their need to be moving, resting only in order to be able to move again, conflicts with the conventions of most classroom and work places, as well as the expectations of many other environments. The ways that hospitals, shelters, detention centres, and courts of law are built represent confinement. All of these create a sense of being caged to a Hunter.

A Hunter embodies ADHD, or what Tribal Theory refers to as 'Attention Directed in a Higher Dimension'. The symptoms of ADHD in the world of mental health are the gifts which a tribal Hunter would require to survive in the wild.

The Hunter is continuously strategizing, and tends to interrupt in conversation. This may create the impression that they are not paying attention, or not listening, but this is often far from the truth. Hunters are almost always paying attention acutely, but only to what they find interesting or pertinent. While listening, they are preparing to do what they may need to do in order to Hunt, or to prevent becoming the hunted themselves.

Hunters are hyper aware of their surroundings and quickly intuit the people around them. These are both abilities that are required to carry out their authentic role.

This awareness and intuition, this ability to see patterns in communication, is uncanny and all too often, hunters know what is going to be said next and jump in in order to 'move' the conversation forward. This alertness and seemingly obstructive attempt to 'get to the point' is the product of decision making abilities and the need to problem solve while in flight or movement. It is acting on impulse, as is often required in flight.

For Hunters, thinking the 'worst first' is an inherent way of being. They see worst case scenarios, and strategize to prevent them. Hunters like to solve problems. They are able to move away from the worst outcome and take measures to prevent the worst from happening. Often extroverted in nature, their intuition allows them to predict and prevent problems. However, if there is no problem to solve, the Hunter will usually create a challenge in order to keep themselves busy and hone these inherent skills.

Hunters need to be connected, holistically, to nature to feed their authentic way of being. The wild one is one with nature, where there are no straight lines, and where unknown danger waits around every bend. The adventurous spirit of the Hunter, in their authentic role, has them 'run to' nature, creating stories and taking risks that both build resilience and cultivate a sense of worth.

WALKABOUT

Tribal theory believes that Hunters carry extra adrenalin in their body systems; they have a built in biological gift which enables them to respond quickly when needed. Hunters will use the expression "I have more gas in the tank". They can push themselves to their limit while in flight.

Flight is the adrenaline response of a Hunter. The ability to call on extra adrenalin is an extremely helpful survival response whether to save oneself or protect the tribe. To run toward the Hunt or to run away from danger.

notes

notes

THE MYTH OF YOUR MISFIT

THE AUTHENTIC HOMEBODY

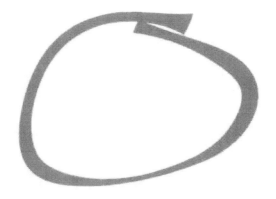

A D D

Attention to Detail Duty

THE AUTHENTIC HOMEBODY

NURTURE & HEART

"the ache for home lives in all of us, the safe place where we can go as we are and not be questioned"

Maya Angelou

A Homebody's Tale

When people say "go to your Happy Place", I immediately think of the blanket forts that I built as a kid. My mom would help me drape huge blankets over the dining room table, and I would keep the chairs tucked in underneath the table, using them as little shelves for the collection of tiny plastic figurines that I got from fast food restaurants. I would gather my stuffed animals and have tea parties or read books out loud, believing that no one, except my stuffed friends, could hear me. I would sing a song about wiggling and I remember laughing to myself so hard that my stomach hurt the next day. That feeling didn't really hurt though; it reminded me of my laughter and it made me smile.

A firefighter's reflection when asked about a childhood safe place.

The Homebody is the nesting heart of the Tribe. The most distinct characteristic of the Homebody is their delight in others, and their comfort in being themselves. They are the nurturers of the heart. They love to love, love to be loved, and do not find purpose in competing with others. They care for others, but, because they like themselves as well, enjoy spending time alone. That time alone is dedicated to discovery; to research, play and create, and to pay attention to details. Homebodies possess the gift of observing details, and, in doing so, acquire the knowledge required to meet the needs of others. The Homebody learns to create an environment for both Hunters and other Homebodies to come to; a safe place to be authentic.

Unlike Hunters, Homebodies do not need to be in constant movement and often prefer to sit in contemplative thought, or to curl up with a book. Homebodies, like hunters, are also intuitive, but their intuition is different. Whereas the Hunter is intuitive with problem-solving', the Homebody is intuitive in 'reading others', and assessing who is friend or foe. This is a protective quality which keeps those who might harm or threaten others away from the safe place. Homebodies are not about problem solving as much as stopping a problem before it starts.

Homebodies are not concerned with crisis management or damage control, but with preventative measures which reduce hypothetical threat; turning unknown danger into manageable risk.

Homebodies do best in a closed environment with other Homebodies and are perfectly capable of communicating with others if brought into a conversation. They are great listeners as this is their way of ascertaining who is and who is not safe. Identifying from the heart, the Homebody can easily give their own heart away if they feel a kinship or trust with someone. If they are corrected or criticized, they exploit the opportunity to grow.

Homebodies require time alone. Unlike the Hunter, who thrives in movement, the Homebody needs to be still and alone to process information, make sense of it, and act upon it. Hunters run; homebodies research.

The Homebody's nesting instincts are strong and Tribal Theory suggests that, although they always had a role in the Tribe in nomadic times, their role of nurturer developed further as humans began to settle in one place for longer periods of time and, in turn, now represent the hearth, the heart, and the home.

No longer required to be continuously on the move, buildings and stable homes became safe places to live, learn, and to land. Thus, the Homebody's place in the Tribe was encouraged to evolve.

Homebodies began to hold community together. Often the quiet participators, they listen and engage and create both a physical and psychological home for others, preparing the nourishment required, and preserving Tribal wisdom through storytelling.

WALKABOUT

People who live on the street are often referred to as Homeless but not all need a roof over their heads to survive. Some need to keep moving to meet the needs of their authentic selves.

Hunters are Hard to House

Homebodies are Homeless

notes

notes

THE GUARD

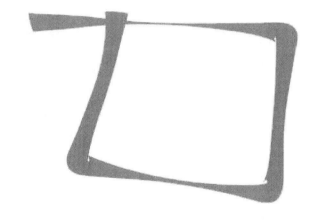

PROTECTOR

THE HEALTHY GUARD

WISE PROTECTOR

"You have the gift of a brilliant internal guardian that stands ready to warn you of hazards and guide you through risky situations"

Gavin de Becker

The amygdalae are two small almond shaped structures (the name comes from the Greek word 'almond' located near the hippocampus in the frontal portion of the temporal lobe in the brain. They initiate the body's response to threat and seem to modulate all our reactions to events that are important to survival.

In Tribal Theory the response to threat is governed by the Guard. Both the Hunter and the Homebody invoke the Guard when threatened. The Guard is what Gavin de Becker, calls "the gift of fear"[1]. It possesses a sensory-like intuition, with an ability to see warning signs and subsequently to prepare survival strategies quickly. It responds to threatening situations with appropriate adrenalin releases that manifest as flight, fight, or freeze responses. As the Healthy Guard responds and solves problems in situations, it builds a foundation of resilience. Resilience can then be called upon when other challenges arise.

When a person is living in their authentic role (homebody or hunter) they will summon what Tribal Theory recognizes as their Healthy Guard. The Healthy Guard is a survival tool, a protector. Without it, our authentic selves would not survive. It is a gift, a primal fear that can only be extinguished with direct consequence.

1. De Becker, G. (1997). *The Gift of Fear*. London: Bloomsbury

THE FEAR GUARD

HYPERVIGILANT PROTECTOR

"You fear that if you lower your guard for even one second your whole world will disintegrate into chaos."

Douglas Coupland

So, what happens if someone is pushed or forced out of their authentic role due to adversity, crises or trauma? (If a hunter is forced to take up a homebody role or vice versa.)

Tribal Theory calls this being DISPLACED.

In forced displacement, under threat, the Healthy Guard is replaced by what Tribal Theory calls the Fear Guard. Having been forced out of their authentic role and place, where a sense of belonging exists, the Fear

Guard usurps the Healthy Guard. The Fear Guard is unable to make meaning of the threatening circumstances and so moves beyond simply trying to protect and fearfully tries to control the environment to keep the tribe safe. In this attempt to control everything, the Fear Guard becomes hyper vigilant, making it difficult to process and make meaning of circumstances. If one cannot make meaning of circumstances, one cannot move out of the Fear Guard, even when a threat diminishes or ends. Displaced, a sense of dis-order is established. One will try to control their environment by attempting to recreate order. When one is displaced from one's authentic self, one cannot recreate or maintain order. This struggle leaves the displaced with the feeling that there is something wrong with them, that they are broken; a misfit.

Unable, in fear guard, to make meaning, protective and natural creative gifts that worked as an authentic Hunter or Homebody, turn into maladaptive responses while displaced. Maladaptive behaviours can present themselves as anxiety, depression, panic attacks, sleep disturbances, ritualized behaviour, self-medicating, self-harm, social disconnection, dissociation, and thoughts of worthlessness. Recognized as disorders in the mental health field, in Tribal Theory, these are symptoms of displacement.

Unable to build resilience while living in Fear Guard, the Displaced person is not existing in their authentic role and therefore cannot tap into the Healthy Guard that makes meaning of and actually solves challenges.

Note: A person can choose to step into a role that is not their natural, authentic role, and function well in what would otherwise be a 'displaced' position if they preserve their authentic selves while doing so.

THE YOUNG HUNTER
FOR CONSIDERATION AND ILLUSTRATION

You began living with your maternal grandmother after your mother died in a ski accident. You were nine years old when the accident happened and although your father was not with your mother at the time of the accident, your maternal grandmother was always referring to how your father failed to protect your mother. In your eyes, this insinuated that it was your father's fault. You and your mother were authentic Hunters; your father, a Homebody. You always recognized and understood the tragic loss that this was to your father and how your grandmother's insinuation that he could not keep his partner safe was devastating to him while you watched him slip further and further into a depression, while your grandmother assumed the role of homebody.

Even at the age of nine you knew that you needed to protect him from your grandmother's blame and shame and you started to stay home more and focus on your father. Spending time with him, trying to be encouraging, doing your best to keep his depression at bay. In doing so, you are displaced. You pull away from your own activities, Hunter games, friends, and adventures to try and control your father's environment to protect him and guard your father. This imposed role creates anxiety as you now spend

42

more time thinking about the bad things that could happen to your father if you were not there to watch over him. The changing of the Healthy Guard to Fear Guard takes hold.

YOUR 'YOUNG' STORY

THE MYTH OF YOUR MISFIT

DISPLACEMENT

Dis-placement

will cause the dis-order,

which presents as different

creative maladaptive behaviours,

showing the dis-ease

affecting the mind, body and soul.

.

THE DISPLACED HUNTER

Trying to force a Hunter to stay still for an extended period will not go well; they will feel confined and trapped.

The natural adrenaline response of a Hunter to being trapped is flight. Physically, they intuitively know how to respond. When pushed into Fear Guard, a Hunter feels backed into a corner. This heightens their flight response which is often misunderstood. It presents itself as oppositional, non-compliant, and defiant. Within institutional environments, the Hunter is often referred to as a 'flight risk'.

The gift of the Hunter is their constant awareness, or Attention Directed in a Higher Dimension (ADHD). In Fear Guard, this presents a psychological and physiological challenge. It is observed as an attention deficit, and hyper dis-order. The Hunter's spiritual nature, however, captured in Fear Guard, will cause the Hunter to feel as though they are now prey.

In Fear Guard, Hunter's present with helplessness

depression, sleep deprivation, consistent heightened awareness, and obsessive and compulsive patterns, which includes repetitive talking.

Disconnecting, unwillingly, from nature for any period of time, the hunter becomes spiritually and physically at dis-ease. They will suffer the same ailments, mentally and physically, as that of a caged animal.

When pushed into Fear Guard, Hunter's present with helplessness and depression; they cannot perform their duty of helping to nourish others. They experience sleep deprivation as their heightened awareness keeps them always alert.

Panic attacks present themselves, accompanied by the feeling of being in a movie, of being watched or watching from the outside, and by tunnel vision. The panic feeling will be marked as a need to run away; to run to.

Physical ailments show up in the lower colon, muscles and nerves. Trapped in Fear Guard, the Hunter presents with dis-eases that are 'hard to pin down' like fibromyalgia and chronic fatigue.

When a displaced Hunter cannot move, they respond in ways that appear maladaptive but are actually the coping strategies springing from attempts to escape from a sense of entrapment, and to carry out their authentic role in the Tribe.

They will find ways to leave their bodies, by wandering, running away in their minds, and dissociating. The Hunter is meeting the need to move, to run 'toward' the Hunt, and to connect spiritually with nature. Connection and interaction with nature is their only way to survive.

THE DISPLACED HUNTER STORY

I loved to play outdoors when I was little. I loved the smell of dirt, wet leaves, and finding that 'perfect' stick. I would come in with my treasures from the backyard and pile them near the back door like a tower of discoveries. I would even sneak out of my bed at night to visit these treasures and go back to bed wondering what I may find tomorrow.

It was dark. I remember that because, when I heard the screaming, I awoke from my sleep and couldn't see anything. It was a terrible scream and it took me seconds to realize that it was my mother. I remember seeing my body moving in front of me, like I was watching myself, as I ran down the stairs. I ran into the kitchen and standing by the back door was a strange man holding my mother, his hand over her mouth, her eyes bulging. He looked me right in the eye, let go of my mother, and ran out the door. My mom fell to the floor and I rushed to her side. She told me to call 911 and I rushed to our wall phone, it was a bright bird's egg blue, and phoned for help. It was the first time that I heard the words 'home invasion'. I remember thinking it made our home sound like a scary place. The police told me how brave I had been, especially at my age, which was seven. I didn't feel brave. I felt changed. I felt that the inside was no longer safe from the outside and that the outside was scary. Like someone was in the bushes or in the trees, watching me. The next day I put on a pair of garden gloves, as to not touch the former treasures which now held the evil of the outside and threw them into a neighbour's leaf pile for them to deal with. I never used the back door again, though I would check it several times every night, three times actually, to make sure it was locked. I stopped playing outside. I hated being inside, but felt unsafe outside. I had a duty now, to be close and protect my mom. Then the night terrors started.

43 year old with former addiction to cocaine and a current sleep disorder

WALKABOUT

Displaced Hunters explode

Displaced Homebodies implode

THE DISPLACED HOMEBODY

When Displaced, Homebodies move inward and blame themselves for failing to keep others safe. They feel responsible to represent home at all times.

In efforts to create family, they work hard to rescue others. Their need to create a safe place is also, in part, a need to belong. In Fear Guard, this desperate effort to engage with others and connect can lead to risky behaviours.

The desire for family-like social connection, for reciprocated intimate connection, can lead to indulgence in alcohol and drugs that enhance social connection, and to exploitive, abusive relationships. A Homebody's response to fear is to freeze physically and emotionally. Because the Homebody processes internally, this dilemma causes a type of generalized anxiety; a 'what if' panic response, as well as feelings of hopelessness and worthlessness.

A Homebody presents with ADD, or Attention to Detail Duty. In their healthy guard, Homebody's role is to pay great attention to who is entering the safe place. When pushed into Fear Guard, ADD is heightened and presents as maladaptive.

A homebody's natural urge to collect and stock up for emergencies and invest in material things which they believe to possess symbolism may turn into hoarding.

Negative self-talk spirals into feelings of hopelessness. Perfectionism is present. Body image issues emerge.

In fear guard, OCD, referred to by Tribal Theory as Only Caring and Daring (and Daring to Care) presents as perseverating thought. The Homebody's, natural gift to intuit and provide for others needs turns inward, into a fear of failing to provide. The Homebody is often capable of conveying an appearance of outward confidence but mercilessly questions themselves internally. Homebodies in Fear Guard will revisit their past words and actions over and over again, in a desperate need not to have done the 'wrong' thing. Their OCD in Fear Guard is again, internal, and creates chants or counting in their heads; often the rituals of choice.

The Displaced Homebody exists in a state of shame. Feeling like a failure for not saving others, they turn on themselves. Unable to fulfill their perceived reason for existence, they wonder why they exist at all. This creates a maladaptive telling of their story. They may cut and burn themselves to experience existence and to release pain. They may reject food and emaciate themselves through eating dis-orders.

The Homebody in Fear Guard attempts to go unseen by others, yet, symbolically, may literally write their stories on their bodies. Frozen thoughts mark their bodies, symbolizing the empathy they wish to create for all.

THE DISPLACED HOMEBODY STORY

I was 22 when we had the fire. My parents were away that night and I had just put my little sister to bed. Our dog, Sassy, was scratching at the basement door; he usually slept down there at night, but was not ready to go to bed. I was really tired and I remember yelling at the dog to go to his bed. I grabbed a blanket and headed for the couch, too tired to do the dishes from the hot chocolate and popcorn we'd had. 'I will do them later' I said in my head.

Frantic barking woke me up. I thought I hadn't opened my eyes, it was so dark with smoke. I could hear my sister crying, she seemed close. I dropped to my knees and crawled, calling out for her. I am told that I was seen dragging her out the front door of the house .I don't remember. The next thing I remember is the smell of bleached hospital sheets and burnt hair.

Luckily my sister and Sassy got out ok. I had dragged my sister out and a neighbor had told the firefighters that we had a dog. They were able to get her out of the basement. In so many ways, Sassy saved all of us, but we lost everything else. Our home was gone.

The firefighter chief had told my parents that the fire had started with the stove being left on. I remember hearing that and shivering with fear. It was my fault. I had caused the fire. I was the reason we lost our home. I could not be trusted. I had not kept my family safe.

38 year old presenting with hoarding behaviour

WALKABOUT

The displaced Homebody will question their self-worth

The displaced Hunter will lose their self-esteem

notes

notes

THE 'MEANING' IN A WORD

"no intervention that takes power away from the survivor can possibly foster her recovery, no matter how much it appears to be in her immediate best interest"

Judith Lewis Herman

THE MYTH OF YOUR MISFIT

Using EVOKE instead of TRIGGER

"As soon as I changed from using the word trigger to using the word evoke, I felt like my cells were dancing with joy, I could begin to heal from the inside, it wasn't about 'out there' anymore"

25 year old sexually assaulted at the age of 14

The term trigger implies that you are responding to something 'outside' of yourself, something you have no control of, an 'out of the blue' thing that has provoked you, something familiar. It provokes feelings associated with a trauma response. The very use of the word 'trigger' may require our amygdala to be on constant guard, hypervigilant, consistently scanning and scoping in an effort to prepare for the unpreparable.

Tribal Theory suggests that the term 'trigger' be replaced with the term 'evoke'. Evoke is from the inside out. It gives the opportunity to prepare and start to take responsibility for how you respond. Knowing you are evoked because of your story, you can make meaning of your response rather than waiting to respond on instinct or impulse alone.

There are many limitations in social work and counselling in efforts not to 'trigger' traumatized individuals. It is nearly impossible to consistently avoid sights, sounds, and words that trigger individuals. Using the term evoke, a person may acknowledge and identify that this is a unique, personal reaction, allowing them to feel less like a victim, and to begin to understand that it is an internal response that they can begin to manage.

Consider these two sentences:

I was so triggered by that scene in the movie last night.

I was so evoked by that scene in the movie last night.

Can you feel a shift?

THE SHOULDERING OF SHOULD

A word commonly found throughout trauma narratives is 'should'.

When we or someone else tells us that we should have done something, we often respond with an uncomfortable twinge. The term 'should' implies that you did wrong, you could have done better, or you made a poor choice; that it is time to doubt yourself; you are looking bad in front of others. 'Shoulds' create an infinite feedback loop of judgement, criticism, and self-blame.

Imagine this word and imagine how it can evoke the cellular memory of those who have grown up or are now experiencing a hyper critical home or environment. There are some people who are more sensitive to the spoken word than others. It may be that through their experiences, their sensitive response is the result of past criticism. It is possible that they may have experienced little else.

The use of this word impacts our belief in our abilities; it evokes doubt. It is a word that can resign us to feel like failures and creates a sense of fragility. It renounces our resilience. Should evokes blame; could evokes strength.

Hurt people hurt people. When we call someone a bully it is not healing. It just adds more hurt to the hurting. It is important to recognize that bullying behavior is a protective behavior. In the lives of many hurt people, it is what has kept them alive. This behavior has kept them focused on how to keep ahead of the game of hurt, and who gets hurt first. It is a strategic and useful game requiring the honing of a strategic mind and real desire to stay alive. It is when the bullying behavior no longer protects someone and they are exposed to the raw hurt they have tragically endured and cannot heal or get support to do so, that they lash out at others or implode on themselves. Reframing bullying as 'exaggerated emotional pain' changes the story.

notes

CHANGING OF THE GUARD

Healthy Guard

to

Fear Guard

"you can't tame the Spirit of someone

who

has Magic in their veins".

unknown

CHANGING OF THE GUARD

HYPERVIGILANT PROTECTOR IN FEAR GUARD

As the Healthy Guard turns into Fear Guard, the Protector turns in a Hypervigilant Protector. This manifests the gifts of the Hunter and Homebody into maladaptive behaviours.

Tribal Theory sees these behaviours as a response to dis-placement, dis-ease and dis-order. In understanding these responses, consider taking away the prefix of these three words and you will note the Healthy Guard, responsible for placement, ease and order, waiting in the wings.

So let's consider a few maladaptive behaviours that again, are gifts, transformed while responding in Fear Guard.

O C D

Only Caring & Daring
(& Daring to Care)

PROTECTING USING MAGICAL THINKING

A CARING AND DARING STORY

I always ran, skipped or jump as a kid. I was told by my family that I would grab my pillow and blanket and sneak out to our back covered porch on summer nights to sleep, and climbing trees made me feel good. One summer evening when I was ten, I was in the backyard digging for something, I don't remember what, when I heard my father yelling, so loud, the loudest I have ever heard anyone yell before. Then a big smash and my little brother's voice screaming "don't, don't Dad, don't", followed by another smash. I don't remember how I got in the house, but I must have run. I remember almost slipping on our kitchen floor and grabbing the corner of the counter. As I steadied myself, I saw my Dad, blood on his hands and broken glass everywhere. I turned and my little brother was curled up in the corner of the room, his hands over his head, his whole body shaking. I saw what had happened. There was the television set, the screen shattered, a bottle sticking out of the screen like it had pierced through from the back of the console. I remember thinking how it looked like a front of a ship, poking through ice. I turned and saw Dad, slouched, as he mumbled something and turned to walk out of the room. He stopped by the entry way and for a moment seemed calm. Then, he punched the wall, so hard his fist went through it. His arm got stuck, and I wanted to help him, but I was too scared, I was afraid he would hit me. He looked at me, his eyes so dark, said "forget this crap" and he went out our front door. I went towards my brother, who was still shaking, I leaned down to put my arms around him and help him up, and as I leaned down, I saw my mother hiding behind the couch. She looked at me. I had never seen her scared, but she looked both frightened and frightening. I have to take care of everyone, I thought. Mom can't do it right now. And it was that night, after I got my little brother to bed, reading him his favourite story, after putting a blanket on my Mom as she fell asleep in her clothes in the big recliner chair, that I went and locked all the doors and windows in the house, scared that my Dad would return the same monster he was when he left. It was that night that I checked the doors and windows three times each. Because I knew there were only three of us now, and I had to keep our home safe from him.

14 year old with outward OCD

THE MAGICAL BRAIN

We know that around nine to twelve years of age, the magical thinking, once the creative part of a child's brain, shifts. If a child has had the opportunity to be in and know their authentic self, this magical thinking develops into healthy, creative thought and exploration. Artistic and scientific minds flourish given the space to do so; magic and the creative mind goes full throttle.

If displaced, a child is in fear guard, this magical thinking, to care for and guard others can turn into 'what if' thinking (in Homebodies) or 'thinking the worst first' (in Hunters). It still shifts into creative thought and exploration, but it is not in joy or curiosity, but survival and caution. This presents itself as OCD, the acronym in Tribal Theory for Only Caring and Daring (and Daring to Care). This acronym is also identifiable as representing Obsessive Compulsive Disorder. Let's look at this disorder from a displacement framework.

Look at our young girl again. We know that she has been pushed into a Homebody role to protect other family members. She is no longer supported to explore and learn her authentic role and is displaced. Never able to be in her authentic role, she may have tried to use her magical thinking to imagine escape routes, visualize a peaceful place she could take her siblings, or even create an imaginary friend to take care of her. As she turns nine, her brain and body, in constant Fear Guard, usurp that magical thinking and instead of developing into joyous creativity, uses it to create magical rituals to keep others and herself safe.

The Fear Guard uses magical thinking and turns it into obsessive thoughts and compulsive behaviour, ways to creatively react in order to keep others safe. OCD develops in order to keep oneself or others safe. "If I tap my toe three times on the school desk leg before I go home, my Dad will not hit my Mom tonight; if my stuffed animals are in a certain order around my head, on my pillow, my Mom will not die; if I do the same routine every day before I get into a car, no one I know will die in an car accident." Obsessive and compulsive behaviour is an attempt to keep yourself and others safe.

If used by the authentic self and the Healthy Guard, this is a gift. It is a disorder, a caring and daring one, if used in Fear Guard.

A DARING TO CARE STORY

It happened so fast. I was sitting in the back of our car watching the rain drops racing each other on the back window. I remember rooting for the tinier drop. Then we were spinning, the whole car, lights swirling around us, a huge red one seemed to follow me like the eye of a monster. Then a heavy feeling on my chest. The moving stopped. I remember I saw the top of my mother's head. Her hair stuck to the roof of the car like it had been glued. I couldn't breathe. I heard sirens. After that I remember a firm, but kind voice telling me I was going to be okay. You and your Mom are okay. I wanted to believe that voice.

For a year after that, anytime I saw anyone get in a car, I felt that if I don't say a quick prayer, something bad would happen to them and it would be my fault. I only do it if it is a red car now. That was the colour of our car that was in the accident, and I only say 'bless you', so it is better.

As far as riding in a car, I refuse to sit in the back. I have to sit in the front, and each time we come to a red light, I look and if someone is standing at the corner waiting to cross I say 'you believe' in my head.

24 year old with inward OCD

MAGICAL THINKING -THE HUNTER IN FEAR GUARD

Because Hunters are naturally outward bound, they will present OCD behaviours outwardly. Their OCD is transparent. It may involve shutting cupboards three times, washing hands over and over, checking and rechecking doors and checking again. Hunters fear that if they don't check and abide by this ritual, someone they care about will be hurt or die.

MAGICAL THINKING -THE HOMEBODY IN FEAR GUARD

Homebodies are internally focused. They will present with OCD behaviours that can't be seen - inner thoughts that stay in hiding. Perseverating thoughts, mantras, chants, imagining they may have hurt someone and not letting go of that fear, re-living a part of the day when they interacted with someone, self-consciously going over and over the conversation hoping they did not say anything wrong that would hurt someone or make themselves look bad.

ANXIETY

&

FEAR GUARD

ANXIETY & FEAR GUARD

We live in a fear-based culture, wherein the Authentic Hunter and Homebody are no longer able to carry out their roles in the Tribe. They are overwhelmed with the belief that they have to be in Fear Guard at all times. This consistent feeling of fear overstimulates the amygdala, and with no resting time to create safety, the Fear Guard remains in charge. Coping skills now become maladaptive as they try to work in a heightened mental fear state.

Fear Guard anxiety is processed and presented differently in the Hunter and the Homebody.

ANXIETY -THE HUNTER IN FEAR GUARD

THINKING THE WORST FIRST

Anxiety for a Hunter is more about a loss of control in their outer environment, and comes and goes.

It presents as a need to control others, specific phobias such as fear of heights and flying (no control) with panic attacks.

When a Hunter has a panic attack, along with general symptoms, the feeling of being 'out of body' is predominant.

ANXIETY -THE HOMEBODY IN FEAR GUARD

MY AMYGDALA NEVER SLEEPS

Anxiety for a Homebody is anxiety that they carry inside themselves.

It presents as social anxiety, social phobia, and generalized anxiety with panic attacks.

When a Homebody has a panic attack along with general symptoms, the feeling of 'not be able to stay calm' is predominant.

notes

notes

HOME
IS WHERE
THE HOARD (HEART) IS

THE HOMEBODY'S CARING HEART BEHIND HOARDING
AN ILLUSTRATION AND CONSIDERATION

A stay at home mother was raising four young children. Her husband, a soldier, had died in war. The husband was an Authentic Hunter and the mother an Authentic Homebody. After the husband's death, the mother, with support, was able work outside the home to keep a living income, and continue to provide a comforting home, a safe place for them to heal and grow. A few years later the oldest son, age 10, got leukemia and, though, medically, everything was put in place, he died. The mother who had been able to endure the loss of her husband and to take on both roles to provide for her children, took the death of her son as a penance, and felt that she had neglected her children by working outside the home. She felt that had she been home more, she would have seen the signs of illness, and been able to provide more nutritious meals. The guilt of not being there consumed her. She was displaced by her husband's death and forced into a Hunter role unable to accept why she had to work, she did not make meaning of her loss. Now, with another loss, and still not able to make meaning, and feeling shamed, she took the blame and created the story that it was her fault. She began to hold on to everything, and her guilt, shame and blame presented itself as hoarding.

When a Homebody, feels that they are not protecting others, their magical thinking, OCD, can present as hoarding. Through hoarding, everything holds a symbolic message of, 'you never know when you might need it'. By holding onto things (many use the term 'packrat') we are keeping (packing) things, in preparation for the next terrible thing that might happen. The Homebody clutters with care and 'feels' their tangible things. Homebodies are natural collectors of items, but when displaced, or having experienced cumulative trauma, they can respond with maladaptive collecting and their anxiety increases if they are asked to 'let go' of anything.

WALKABOUT

DIS-order   ORDER

DIS-ease   EASE

DIS-placed   PLACE

notes

"my cells felt like they were dancing"

workshop participant

HEALING STORIES

TO THINE OWN PLACE BE TRUE

"we shall not cease from exploration, and the end of all of our exploring will be to arrive where we started and know the place for the first time "

T.S. Eliot

When you come to know your authentic self, your Fear Guard subsides. You are then able to re-tell your story and make meaning of your experiences and celebrate your role in the Tribe.

THE HEALING STORY OF A HUNTER

About two and a half years ago I heard about the Tribal Theory. I fell into the 'hunter' category. Things became very clear to me. Many obstacles that I had experienced in life were a result of me having to stand in other positions. Let me explain.

My parents separated when I was 3. Soon after, my mother, my older sister and I moved to the city. After my parents divorced, I found myself 'struggling' to find where I fit in. My sister was there to look after me, while my mom was working two jobs. But I wasn't happy. I felt that I was in the way and a nuisance. So I gave myself a job to protect my mom and sister. Looking back now and being able to identify what I was feeling, was "on guard". As we grew older, that task got harder. My sister started hanging out with her friends more and my mom was still working. This was when I found my love for the outdoors. I loved going out bike riding, hiking, farming with my grandparents and exploring the world around me. Unable to find a happy place or a good balance, I left home for the streets. I was panhandling, squatting, and partying for a few years. This caused a lot of problems at home. Through family mediation, I was able to come home. sobered up and started working. In my early 20's, I started my career in the building trades as a Heating and Air Conditioning mechanic. I felt that this was the job for me. Going to different places and having to seek, investigate and navigate, mostly outdoors, and talking to people. It had all of the elements that I needed and wanted in daily activities and future endeavours. It only took 6 years of trade school to become fully licensed. And I did it. But not everything was a great as it should have been. I was in an unhealthy relationship. I now found myself as the "homemaker." This was a very difficult time for me. I had a lot of anger and resentment towards him. And there was a lot of fighting.

After I left him, I heard about Tribal Theory. And there it is! I am a "Hunter". This best describes who I am on the inside. I am the person that needs space and likes to stay active. I am Always up for adventure.

When I was young, I stood in the guard mode, which I could do for a while, but I was very unhappy and unsettled. As I grew older, I stood in the homemaker mode. Which, again I could do, but I still needed more than that. A hunter needs to hunt.

Now that I understand this theory and how it applies to me, I feel that I am at peace with myself because I can be myself; my Authentic Me. And I know that I can do those other tasks, but I need to keep true my Authentic Self. When I am having unsettled days, then I know that it is adventure time. It's time for me to be me. For me, I know that if I push this aside that I can lose myself in the process. Having to stand in the other positions for a while, I feel a greater understanding for those around me. It has helped me in my judgments of others and how I interact with them.

We are all different. We all have a different story. We all come from different places and we all have different heartache or events in our stories. If we could see that we naturally play a role in our community then maybe we could stop being so critical of each other. And we can learn to help, teach and accept each other in the best way possible, as we stand in our authentic places.

A former street kid now a tradesperson

THE HEALING STORY OF A HOMEBODY

I took A Tribal Theory workshop and had an "aha moment" about my childhood. Growing up with an alcoholic father, I realized that due to my true (homebody) nature I experienced a lot of mental stress. I avoided home on weekends when my dad would drink excessively, and I felt guilty for leaving my mother and younger sister as they walked on eggshells to avoid my father's anger and belligerence. I wanted to be at home in my room, having friends over like kids on TV did. But the truth was, it was not a safe place. So, I always found somewhere else to go. This fear and restlessness resulted in me engaging in teenage drinking and other risky behavior to manage my feelings and medicate my pain. I was not being true to my inner nature but I had difficulty expressing it. Taking this workshop in Tribal Theory confirmed to me that there are all sorts of reasons people act out in ways that are not conducive to who they really are. This reaffirmed the importance of making my home a haven for not only my family, but also for my children's friends who spend time here.

A Front Line Crisis Worker

WALKABOUT

Once you see that healing is about being in your authentic 'place,' it is like pulling a thread. You know that something is happening. There is a baseline shift, a ripple effect, and the meaning of that shift infiltrates all of the stories of who you are and what happened to you. It re-aligns the whole story - the thread becomes a lifeline.

notes

A HEALING PRACTICE

THE TRAUMA LIFE LINE
&
THE HEALTHY GUARD LINE

THE TRAUMA LIFE LINE & HEALTHY GUARD LINE

"The cave you fear to enter holds the treasure you seek"

Joseph Campbell

As Tribal Theory evolved, I developed tools to help individuals uncover and explore their authentic place in the Tribe and to begin to identify and unravel the events and circumstances of their past that had most significantly shaped their life choices and consequent outcomes. Understanding why they thought what they thought and did what they did, viewed through the new lens that Tribal Theory offers, provides many of the missing pieces of the puzzle that begins to clarify and make meaning of how they arrived at where and who they are now.

Two of these simple tools have proven to be very powerful in this respect and they work in tandem to reveal valuable insights that in and of themselves often prove to be helpfully transformative. One is the Trauma Life Line and the other is the Healthy Guard Line.

HOW TO CREATE
THE TRAUMA LIFE LINE & HEALTHY GUARD LINE

The easiest way to illustrate and understand these tools is to apply them to your own life story.

1. On a piece of blank paper, in the landscape position, draw a single straight line across the paper from left to right, about 1/3 of the way from the top.
2. Label this line the 'the Healthy Guard Line'.
3. Draw a second straight line across the paper from left to right, parallel to the first line and about 2/3rds of the way from the top.
4. Label this line the 'Trauma Life Line'
5. Write 'birth' on the left and 'now' on the right of each of these lines.

Healthy Guard Line

birth_____now

Trauma Life Line

birth_____now

YOUR TRAUMA LIFE LINE & HEALTHY GUARD LINE

WALKABOUT

Many of our childhood memories about ourselves come from other people's stories. We often carry these stories and believe them to be the true reflection of who we are. However, they may not be.

Tales told to us of our strengths, gifts and wisdom shape us differently than those pointing out our weakness, failures and lack of awareness.

The stories told to us, about us, by others, can have a strong influence on how we began and continue to perceive ourselves.

USING THE TRAUMA LIFE LINE

The Trauma Life Line is where we are asked to tell our unique story. In Tribal Theory, these are the answers to the who, what, where, and why questions. Who do you think hurt you? What did you do to survive? Where did you feel safe? When did you start guarding yourself and others? And when you see the Why, it will be time to change your story.

Starting with the Trauma Life Line, try to remember experiences or events in your life that seemed to have a disruptive or negative impact on you or that you would consider as a crisis or traumatic event.

Write a short label or phrase that represents the experience on the Trauma Life Line at the place that most closely represents the age in your life (between your birth and now) when this experience, or these experiences, occurred.

Continue identifying and marking events where you responded traumatically on the Trauma Life Line until you are satisfied that you have recorded the 'main events' that you can remember at this point in time. Don't worry about the neatness or any specific order.

This is more of a jam session than a recording session.

(Note for those of you counseling clients. They may find identifying with one event is enough in your session with them. You can always pick it up where you left off next time you see them or they can take it with them and ad on when they are ready.)

The Trauma Life Line is a way to assist you in telling 'your' story about the challenging events that have had adverse effects on your life. It becomes a 'safe place' for you to monograph your experiences and it can be helpful whether or not you have yet identified with an Authentic Tribal role. Many times, in fact, it may help you to discover and clarify what your role is likely to be.

THE SENSE-ABLE STORY

It is quite common to put the first mark of our stories on the line at the age where we consciously remember, around the ages of four to six. If you do not remember your early childhood, start in your older childhood.

Sometimes, you may be baffled because you cannot recall anything traumatic that has happened to you. You may believe that you were fortunate to have a healthy family and/or community environment which supported your growth and that you have made meaning of adverse events in your life, yet you still feel dis-placed.

This is when asking yourself about your birth, childhood illnesses, or events that happened before you could talk (from your non-verbal years) can be helpful as you may have a 'sense able' story to tell. These trauma responses are imprinted in your sensory memory and can prove enlightening as you may not have considered the possible impact of these events. You will carry these events as sensory responses. You had no words to cognitively tell the story of what happened, and your senses can tell and keep the story, not just in the brain, but stored in the cells all over your body. (this is often referred to as cellular memory)

When you are able to attach 'sense' responses to experiences, and then to a narrative, your seemingly impulsive responses are no longer impulsive and you will be 'able' to make meaning of your story.

Tribal Theory calls it the 'sense able' story.

"So maybe this is why I feel this way around needles and get a headache and panicky whenever I even think about them."

16 year old who was hospitalized for first three months of their life as a preemie and gets anxious and has panic attacks when walking past clinics or hospitals.

Every mark on the Trauma Life Line is a chapter in your story, a bread crumb marking a trail, acknowledging and validating your experiences. It is an opportunity to gain insight into what actually has happened to you and will help you make sense of your dis-order, dis-ease, and feelings of dis-placement. It will help you to step back with order, ease and placement and to look at your life, and connect with the parts that have left you feeling like a misfit.

A client once said "it is like looking at my life as a canvas and I am finally able to paint the picture of what has happened to me, and not what is wrong with me"

The Trauma Life Line is a line of self-inquiry that emerges from the inside out. Because you are recalling and recreating your own story, you will uncover and express what you want or innately need to reveal.

(As caregivers and counsellors we become witnesses, not judges, of these unfolding revelations).

WALKABOUT

Non-verbal hurt, which is hurt experienced when one was non-verbal, is nevertheless stored in the cells of our body.

Our cells hold the memories of the event.

Experiences prior to mastering language are kept here.

Telling the story through a therapeutic sensory model will be more effective than through a narrative, as there were literally 'no words' to express or connect to the event(s)

notes

THE HEALTHY GUARD LINE

The Healthy Guard Line helps to reveal an alternative story from the point of view of your in born healthy guide. It is told by the part in all of us that was called upon to find creative ways to survive when our lives or safety were threatened by someone or something in our past. In Tribal Theory, it is the inner creativity of the Authentic Self, and guided wisdom connected to the Healthy Guard. It is the part of us that recognizes our ability to nurture, and our connection with nature.

In Tribal Theory, making meaning, connection, safety and belonging are primary pillars in healing from crisis or trauma. As you consider the different trauma responses to events identified on the Trauma Life Line, you use the parallel line (the Healthy Guard Line) to consider and mark how your Authentic self with the Healthy Guard tried to help you in your times of need.

This is where you can shift the Trauma Life Line story into one of caring, bravery, and resilience. As you see how you were able to call on your Authentic Self and Healthy Guard to guide you through difficult and challenging times, you will simultaneously begin to write a new story of how you did the best you could under the circumstances.

You will also be able to connect with that part of yourself that has always been present. This Authentic Self and Healthy Guard are the parts of yourself that helped you through. Working through this process, we gain a greater understanding of how connection is so very important to us as humans. Tribal Theory suggests that it is very difficult, if not impossible, to connect in a healthy and productive way with ourselves and others or to make meaning of what has happened if we are displaced. When someone is given the opportunity to discover and to really see their Authentic Self and Healthy Guard Line, they are able to connect with this part of themselves. This connection then makes it possible to interconnect other experiences they have struggled with and endured and to begin to tell the whole story that illuminates how they tried to serve their family, themselves, and others. The new version of their story will clearly demonstrate how they tried to keep a connection with others in any way that they could, and how their Authentic Self, even displaced, was still able to call up their Healthy Guard Line.

The Healthy Guard Line can show up in different ways to different people. Some will have had an imaginary friend when they were little, others will describe a welcoming voice in their minds, others a feeling of protection. People who have forgotten about their guide are now able to bring forth some amazing stories of their own strength and endurance and recognize their own personal resilience.

Post traumatic dis-order becomes post trauma growth; victims become survivors and a survivor can thrive as they self-identify with their new story and connect with therapeutic healing models that resonate with their Authentic role in the Tribe.

A LINE DRAWN MAKES MEANING
ILLUSTRATION & CONSIDERATION

There is a young man in his early 30's who finds it difficult to go back to work after a flood that occurred in his office. It happened in the basement of the building where he works and his office is on the first floor. When the flood happened he and other co-workers evacuated the building and no one was hurt, or, in the man's perception, was bothered much by it. However, when he went to return to work he found that as soon as he got close to the building he experienced a panic attack. He felt he could not breathe, his teeth clenched and he felt disconnected. These panic feelings continued to happen each day for several days and so he went to the hospital. He was diagnosed with anxiety and it was suggested he consider counselling.

This man identified as an Authentic Homebody. While doing his Trauma Life line, he related different things that he had encountered that he considered traumatic. He started relating stories about his adolescent years and then suddenly lowered his voice and whispered that, during his childhood, around the age of seven, his mother had been in a car accident. I asked if he would be comfortable talking about it further. He continued, now in his normal tone, and said that it had left his mother physically disabled and immobile. She started drinking heavily. He said they lived in a rancher house, with no upstairs, just a basement. When she would drink, his mother would get very angry and yell a lot. His father, after a couple of years of trying to understand his mother's frustration and drinking to feel better, would often not come home from work until she had passed out from drinking. This left him, as a boy, to come home from school to take care and deal with his mother's emotional outbursts. He told the story about how he would go to the basement, which was always damp, and hide. Telling his mother he was going out to be with friends, but knowing he could not leave her alone, he would go to the basement with comics and a flashlight. He could hear his mother above, so he would be aware if she fell or hurt herself. He felt scared at times, but also felt it was the right thing to do.

By telling the story and now being aware of his sensory memories, he connected the smells of the basement with the flood at work. It had evoked the feelings he felt when he had to be so quiet in the basement, in the dark, scared for his mother and always paying attention to every little noise, in case the 'stranger', as he referred to his mother when she was intoxicated, came alive in the house. He began to connect his physiological responses to his cellular memories of being pushed into the Fear Guard role; a Homebody with no safe place or ability to create one. The flood had literally brought a 'flood' of memories to the surface. He had found meaning in his panic attacks. In drawing the Healthy Guard Line over his Trauma Life Line he was able to look at what his Healthy Guard had been doing. He discovered that his Healthy Guard within himself had a caring, understanding and empathetic nature.

As a young boy, he had tried to care for his mother, and understood that his father had to stay away. This included, empathizing with his mother's loss of mobility in the car accident, empathy for his father's loss of a partner and an awareness of his own innate bravery in coming forth and doing his best, while displaced, to take care of the situation.

He went on further to connect this displacement with the maladaptive behaviours that surfaced in his adolescents. His panic attacks subsided and he returned to work.

notes

notes

"these mountains that you are carrying,
you were only supposed to climb."

Najwa Zebian

RESILIENCE
&
SUR-THRIVAL

WHAT ABOUT RESILIENCE?

A child who has been able to explore and develop their authentic self will build a strong sense of self-worth. With the addition of healthy nurturing, a second advantage is realized; the gift of resilience. Why is nurturing so important? As a child explores their authentic self, they are guided by nature, whether they are a Hunter, rolling in the dirt, tasting ants, climbing objects, or a Homebody, building bed sheet forts, sorting and placing stuffed animals, helping to cook. If a child makes a mistake while taking on these natural draws, a nurturing caregiver will not criticize. They will turn it into a learning moment. This acceptance encourages a child to become confident in their natural interests and abilities and know they can problem solve and resolve when making mistakes.

What if that child is not allowed to grow in their authentic role? What if the child is not nurtured, but criticized, shamed, or blamed? This child has a lesser chance of developing resilience because this child lives in the position of the Fear Guard.

This place is where children feel like 'misfits', 'castaways', 'lost'. They have little, if any, resilience because anytime they have tried to solve a problem, criticism has made them feel like failures. They don't believe that they can 'weather the storm,' and all too often feel they are actually the cause of it.

I do not believe that children are born resilient. Nor do I believe that children, in time, will naturally 'get over it'. The body remembers and the spirit can be diminished. Displaced, a child does not get over it, a child learns to live 'in' it.

I am often asked about children who are able to be in their authentic role and not criticized, yet are also not given healthy instructions on how to resolve mistakes or problems, and are left to their own devices. These children will do well on the outside, yet consistently seek validation in relationships, presenting as strong individuals but feeling lost without the acknowledgment of others.

This is difficult for the authentic self because it has learned to 'doubt', and this, in turn, can lead to difficulties in decision making.

Nevertheless, even after years of not being able to be your authentic self and/or not being granted the gift of resilience through external nurturing, the simple action of identifying your authentic self and understanding that you were pushed or forced into a fear guard position can create a paradigm shift in how you see yourself and the world and then move towards taking steps towards healing and well-being.

SUR-THRIVAL

Certain adverse events can be stressful. The way that we respond can be identified as a crisis response or post-traumatic stress. This can move to post traumatic stress dis-order if not mitigated using tools to develop meaning and self-understanding. If we can make meaning, we are able to move towards post-traumatic growth.

Be aware when someone is telling their story of what has happened to them and, using Tribal Theory roles, try to connect with their authentic selves. In doing so, often a person is able to call on their Healthy Self to begin to see adverse events through a different lens, a lens that shows them the map of survival, and a road to follow in order to thrive. To sur-thrive.

FOR THE LOVE OF A 'SILL-Y' CAT
AN ILLUSTRATION AND CONSIDERATION

I didn't know what to do. The fire had consumed the whole house. People were so generous giving me things, and the other tenants too. I was lucky to be alive I kept telling myself, over and over again. But I couldn't stop shaking and it didn't help that every time I breathed in through my nose I could still smell, 'burnt'. I decided to meet with someone, who had been offered by victim services in our community. I figured maybe they could tell me something that would help these pictures in my head turning over and over again, especially of the cat. My cat had been carried out by my neighbour, since I was carried out on a gurney. I had broken my leg two weeks earlier. The cat I couldn't get out of my head was the alley cat that used to sit on my window sill, only when the window was closed. I had fed him for about three months and the way he would look at me through the window, his eyes open wide, almost like he was smiling through them. I had named him 'Silly', lame I know, but I felt like my window 'sil' was his home. My own cat totally ignored him. She showed no interest or jealousy when I would feed him. I like to think she knew he just needed someone and that someone was us. Since the fire, I could not get the picture of Silly's eyes out of my mind. They were imprinted on the back of my eyelids. I was worried about where he was, who would feed him, and worse, that he might have died. I was hesitant to go see someone.

Talking about my feelings was not something I usually did, and to be honest, I didn't know how I felt, just not right. So, I went. I was introduced to someone who called themselves a crisis and trauma counsellor. I thought, okay, trauma really? I remember the counsellor asking me about the fire by remembering through sounds, smells and touch, quite odd I thought, but I was amazed how much I was able to tell them, as I had tried to remember things since the fire but was unsuccessful. Frozen, was the way it was described by the counsellor, and that is the way it felt. I was also asked about things I like to do, how I like to spend my time, and things like that and what had been happening to me since the fire. This counsellor explained the role of a Hunter and the role of a Homebody and I quickly identified with the Homebody. When I was asked about animals I connect with, I started to cry. Sob, actually. And then I talked about 'Silly'.

It wasn't long until it hit me...the impact of worrying about Silly. I didn't know where he was, so in a sense, 'my sense' everyone was not safe, someone was still missing. I realized within moments that as a Homebody, this would be devastating to me, and until I found out what happened, I would not rest. There was no guarantee I would ever find Silly and the counsellor asked me what I might consider doing to honour Silly and our time together. I answered without hesitation, help other cats. And that is what I did. As soon as I applied to work for a cat shelter, the eyes of Silly no longer haunted me. I work there permanently now, after two years of volunteering. Every time a cat comes in, I thank Silly for sending them to me.

I know, it is obvious I didn't find Silly. My hope is that he has found another window sill, but if not, if he did die, I envision him in cat heaven, building a treehouse with a window and sill to sit on. I know now, that by doing what my Authentic Homebody would do and listening to the guidance of my Healthy Guard I was able to move forward with a purpose and make some meaning of what happened.

31 year old former assistant daycare teacher now an animal rescuer

WALKABOUT

Addictions present to cope with trauma. They are a spiritual crisis, a yearning to find your authentic self, place and purpose.

They are used to try and reach, touch, taste and feel the authentic self from a place of displacement.

Most addictions come from accumulated trauma.

It is the constant requirement to be in Fear Guard that creates an 'addict'...they are actually 'addicted' to finding meaning to survive

notes

.

SELF HARM
THE PRACTICE OF SPIRITUAL HEALING

"I feel like a ghost until I feel the sting and the warmth then I think maybe I'm me"

17 year old who 'cuts'

Displaced Hunters and displaced Homebodies use self-harm to try and move from displacement. It is a symbol of spiritual crisis, and the ritual of a 'lost soul'. The cellular pain they experience evokes primal gestures like cutting, burning, and bone breaking to try to connect with their soul.

Tribal Theory provides an alternative approach to addressing and understanding non-suicidal self-injury. Using the framework to acknowledge the story of how the soul was misplaced, (in present time or in preceding generations) it allows individuals to re-tell their story.

In doing so, the soul is awakened, as it was never lost.

INTERGENERATIONAL TRAUMA

ECHOES OF THE ELDERS

"Our Ancestors knew that healing comes in cycles and circles"

Gemma B. Benton

Tribal Theory operates on the idea that our body remembers. We now know that memories are stored in cells all over our body and that our cellular memories are influenced by our environment and carry that influence in to subsequent generations. Regarding trauma, this is known as intergenerational trauma.

Tribal Theory uses the retelling of your story to shift intergenerational trauma. By telling your cells a different story (a story of survival and resilience,) trauma carried by cells from a prior generation or generations is given new meaning and, with this meaning, trauma shifts and is reattached to cells as historical tales, not terrors. In the retelling of the story, the Fear Guard steps down and the Healthy Guard steps in.

The Authentic Self is acknowledged as are the authentic selves of those who experienced the trauma carried via DNA. The cellular memory carries trauma from generation to generation, waiting until that trauma story is revealed and retold by the Healthy Guard. The changing of the guard takes place as soon as we can make meaning.

This is why the Healthy Guard above the Trauma Life Line is so important. When retelling the story through the Healthy Guard, you are retelling the story to every cell in your body (to your cellular memories). Tribal Theory believes, by doing so, you change the past, present and future at a cellular level. We now have a purpose, a way to begin healing the past, present and future as well.

Tribal Theory responds to the echoes of the Elders in asking those who feel helpless and hopeless to acknowledge their authentic role of healer, which has been honoured to them from the peoples and stories of the past.

By exploring the ways to connect with their authentic selves, a Hunter or Homebody can access the medicine of the Healthy Guard, to support and heal themselves and others. In doing so, there is purpose. In being so, there is meaning.

Tribal Theory provides a framework in which all therapies have a place. Many therapies will work best for Hunters. Others will work best for Homebodies. Helping individuals to find their authentic place in their tribe is the first crucial step for both helpers and those seeking help.

TRIBAL THEORY IS A CANVAS FOR ALL THERAPIES

IN THE ART OF HEALING.

TRIBAL THEORY MEETING PLACE

FAMILY MATTERS

"I have three kids; two are Homebodies and one is a Hunter. I am a dog person and I began seeing that it is like having two yellow Labs and a Jack Russel, and instantly I was able to change my parenting for the better"

Parent and Emergency Nurse

CLASS 'WITH LOTS OF' ROOM
TO BE YOUR AUTHENTIC SELF

"I use Tribal Theory in my class to help students identify their authentic roles and then teach to those roles.

My classroom is now a place of learning, with students focused on their studies while striving towards emotional well-being for each other and themselves...Tribal Theory is a simple miracle!"

Grade 7 Teacher

CHANGING MY WORLD

"Until learning about Tribal theory, I was always pushing my husband to do things I wanted but against his will. I was always pushing him to do what a Hunter would do. I asked him to go out there and get extra work, travel to unfamiliar places, have new experiences, and to try new things with a strong and daring heart, regardless of the consequences. Thirty-three years of marriage didn't get us anything but more arguments and conflict.

I was so lucky to get the Tribal Theory Training. It brought an end to our misunderstanding of each other.
The first thing I considered in the workshop was where do I fit into this and who am I?

Hunter, Homebody, sometimes both? How does that work? Sometimes I am Martha Stewart and other times I am Indiana Jones. So, am I a hunter and homebody at the same time?

I went back into my own deep history to analyze why I'm this way. After much thought, I realized that at first I was forced to be a Homebody based on the cultural perspective that believes that the best place for a woman is in the home. After ten years of marriage I had my first babies. I had complications during the births so I chose to stay home. I chose to always be around and not to leave them as result of fear and to protect them.

There was always an urge inside me to work, to do

anything and anywhere. I always kept myself calm and convinced myself that I needed to be home to keep my kids in a safe environment. By understanding how Tribal Theory works and applying it to myself, I have come to understand myself better. It helped me put colors on the black and white pictures of my life.

Now, I clearly understand that I'm a Hunter, not a Homebody. I made choices under specific circumstances, that made sense to me at the time, but now I know who I am.

I have started a new phase of my life focussed on being true to myself.

Tribal Theory has also helped me understand my children's behavior and their true personalities.

As a counsellor, it has had a huge impact on me as it has helped me understand my client's souls.

As an entrepreneur it has impacted the way I choose my employees and the way I run my business. It has empowered me and increased my confidence.

As a Community Facilitator, welcoming refugees and new immigrants to a new country, Tribal Theory helps me better understand everyone's behaviour. It helps us understand the best way to deal with and resolve any conflicts and other challenges we face.

As a writer who is working on culture shock to develop strategies for immigrants and refugees the training has helped me in my efforts to better understand where they came from and find better ways to work around it.

Last, but not least, Tribal Theory has helped me 'feel

the vibe' with everyone I meet or work with, and creates an easy flow between myself and others."

Immigrant and Refugee Settlement Worker

'this simple, practical front line field theory is like having a psychological AED for trauma & response in your pocket... amazing!'

BC Paramedic

TO SERVE AND PROTECT

"There are endless benefits both personally and professionally to understanding tribal theory, even at its most basic level.

Because of tribal theory I have a better understanding of who I am and how I fit into this world as an individual, a family member, a friend, a co-worker. Personally, tribal theory has redefined my past and provided a different perspective for the future.

My past, wrought with personal crisis and professional confliction, is reframed with the understanding of my genuine place within my tribe. Self-blame, doubt and low self-esteem is replaced with true understanding, contentment and self-awareness. The puzzle pieces of life seem to fit better and for longer.

My future choices are made with the education and awareness of my valued place and as naturally as the seasons change, happiness always finds me –my true self.

So many of us are forced into roles/jobs/careers due to outside pressures, expectations and commitments. The majority are not happy and can never figure out why. The simple answer based on tribal theory is that we are outside of our natural roles. We are trying to fit a round block into a square hole.

Working in the police industry, I am now instinctively aware of those colleagues who are in their defined role as a hunter or a guard and those who are forcing the round block into the square hole. It does not come as a surprise that those who are forcing the pieces are also in regular conflict with their peers and supervisors.

As a victim services worker, I am able to have an insight into my clients' genuine place within the tribe. I am able to better craft coping skills and methods based on this, even if they are unaware of tribal theory. I am able to help them succeed and move past trauma utilizing tribal theory insights."

Victim Services Coordinator with the police

"Your place in the Tribe is where you thrive"

Barbara Allyn

ABOUT THE AUTHOR

Barbara Allyn is a certified trauma therapist and crisis intervention worker with 25 years of active front line crisis response. As a highly respected and sought after facilitator, she brings a wealth of experience from her work as a family mediator, adolescent clinical counsellor, and classroom behaviour specialist. Barbara originated and advances the unique, creative trauma-response model - Tribal Theory, which is being embraced by the international trauma and crisis community. The theory is being described by frontline responders, counsellors and teachers, as easy to apply, practical and a very effective healing model to post-traumatic growth and well-being. Barbara lives with her husband in Vancouver, BC, Canada

to find out about booking workshops or speaking
events please contact:

website: www.tribaltheory.org

or call

778-297-9398

facebook: Tribal Theory Meeting Place
twitter: @tribal_theory

Tribal Theory
Ste 101
185-9040 Blundell Road
Richmond, BC V6Y 1K3
Canada

Made in the USA
Columbia, SC
27 August 2017